Avec nos meilleurs sentiments
et notre profonde Considération

Pierre et Nadine BOURGIN.

Sébastien Griffe

DISCOVER
LYON
AND ITS WORLD HERITAGE

EDITIONS
LA TAILLANDERIE

COLLECTION PLURIEL

Edited by Gérald Gambier

Photographs and captions :

Gérald Gambier

Infography : Patricia Graizely
Translation : Sophie Maraux - Hedwige West

© Editions La Taillanderie - 2003
rue des frères Lumière
01400 Châtillon-sur-Chalaronne
Tél : 04 74 55 16 59
Fax : 04 74 55 14 27
contact@la-taillanderie.com
www.la-taillanderie.com

broché - ISBN 2-87 629-267-X
relié - ISBN 2-87629-268-8
ISSN en cours

Contents

INTRODUCTION

To describe a town, one must not only show its assets and distinctive features but also the character of its inhabitants and their failings. It is the same for a town as it is for a person : one must tolerate its flaws or mistakes, in order to have a mature and broad- minded understanding.

Clichés that come to mind when we think of Lyon's inhabitants are their notorious taste for secrecy : Félix Benoît defines Lyon as "*a town where people laugh like they make love : in private*", and their desire for recognition which, at one time, fuelled the frustration of not being the capital of the country.

The water tournaments, specific to Lyon, inherited from the Nautes and from the Rhône rescuers.

Much to the chagrin of some people, Lyon imposed itself in many domains. Lyonese people are quite capable of being the best at what they do if they want to. Very often, aspects that are the least promoted are the

The second-hand book dealers on the bank of the Saône: perhaps our last reminder of the glory of sixteenth century Lyonnais printing.

From Fourvière Hill, chimneys standing out against Croix-Rousse Hill.

most successful : such is the case for Lyonese jewellery which swamped the market in France. The same can be said for chemistry and pharmacy which will soon be recognized as the World Center of Transmitted Disease Control and Warning is set up after the European Center of Virology.

Lyon's fame is also due to past glories.

First of all, the city is known for its gastronomy, not only because it is considered a true Lyonese tradition and even a form of art, but also because the Ambassador of French Cuisine, Paul Bocuse, was born in Lyon and created one of the most prestigious culinary competitions in the world there.

Lyon is also known for its silk weaving. While this tradition has been unable to keep up with industrialisation, the exceptional quality of the silk is still vaunted by Haute-Couture designers, and its unique construction in terms of single fiber weaving is used by even the highest forms of technology today.

The Resistance itself knew how to make the most of the short months of respite when Lyon was part of the Free Zone by taking advantage of the town's position on the Saône and Rhône valleys. Jean Moulin's martyrdom is an emblem for Lyon.

As part of the new attractions, the painted walls should be mentioned (one hundred and fifty all in all have invaded Lyon's walls and its suburbs). Also, the Lights Project which began on the December 8th Celebration, and was subsequently extended to the 365 nights of the year illuminating 270 sites. Finally, the city's dance community is gaining recognition, due in part to the Biennal Dance Festival which gathers all of France's best dancers and even attracts outstanding dance troups from around the world.

The people of Lyon now look forward to the street parade at the Biannul Dance Festival. Photo : Martine Leroy.

To top it off, on 5 December 1998, Unesco registered Lyon as a World Heritage Site, thus acknowledging the historical and architectural worth of the city and classifying it as part of the world's wonders.

Lyon failed to see the importance of the cinema. As opposed to the Lumière brothers who invented it, Lyon did not think it wise to exploit it and let it develop elsewhere for over one hundred years. The centenary went by unnoticed, and only one of the numerous painted walls relates the story. It was only at the end of the 20th century that people started to find some interest in the site where the first film was shot by including it within the new buildings of a real film industry institute, instead of tearing it down with the rest of the Lumière factories. Today, Lyon recognizes the aura of the Cannes festival and regrets not having its own festival. It did let the opportunity slip by and yet, it may not be too late to catch up.

At the Mère Cottivet bouchon, the love of the Lyonnais boule is used as an excuse for a very 'Canut' decor.

If the same determination that was used for the Lumière Project is developped in Lyon, a ceremony like the "*Golden Lyon Awards*" given at the Venice festival or the "*Lumière Awards*" could well take place in Lyon at the site where the first film was shot. It would be considered so prestigious !

Lyon has changed and is still changing on account of the work of two local councils which took great care on insisting on that the town's development be based on its own riches and strengths. It can be said that in the third millenium, Europe will have to take this city into account, regardless of what some may think, because of its unique value.

The story of a city is sometimes very similar to the tale entitled "*The Ugly Duckling*". Once upon a time, there was a town called Myrlingue where two rivers were flowing and which was drowned in fog. At that time, it possessed magnificent Gallo-Roman monuments on Fourvière Hill but they were used as a stone quarry for the building of the cathedral.

During the Renaissance, Italian bankers and merchants started constructing next to the great medieval cathedral with a vengeance. Progressively, the town covered new ground without destroying its

The large rosace by Jacques de Beaujeu on the façade of Saint John-the-Baptist's Primatial church.(1392).

The Singing School (12th century) contains the treasure of the cathedral.

Bacchus'drunkenness.
A mosaic from the Gallo-Roman Civilisation Museum of Fourvière Hill.

architectural heritage. Most buildings were erected within the Peninsula during the 17th, 18th, and 19th centuries. Then Croix-Rousse Hill was used to accommodate the Canuts silk workers who possessed the new Jacquard mechanical looms.

These extensive historic changes within the city itself are still noticeable today around every street corner and enable us to be in direct contact with the changes brought about as centuries have gone by. For Unesco experts, this was of paramount importance under standing that the town was to be part of the World Heritage.

The town's architectural wealth was so eye-catching that some people felt that Lyon was worth renovating. When this heritage had been sufficiently shown to its advantage, it seemed that Lyon really deserved to belong to Unesco. Only the old city center, the Medieval district and the Renaissance period were concerned. Yet Unesco experts were so much under the town's spell that they encouraged the people in charge of the inscription dossier to include every single one of the historic districts – that is to say 10% of the city itself – with Old Lyon, Fourvière Hill, Saint Just, Croix-Rousse Hill and 3/4 of the Presqu'île Peninsula.

Being part of the World Heritage Sites is due to the readability of historic epochs across the city's monuments.

Draperer Thomassin's house on Place du Change (15th century).

In Saint-Martin-d'Ainay's church, the four imposing Egyptian pillars which astounded Rabelais.

On Croix-Rousse Hill, a 19th century Canut building.

For each area, the cultural, human and architectural heritage was considered. This explains why, on Croix-Rousse Hill – classified as *"Heritage Protection Site"* since 1994 -, the skills of the Canuts are as valuable as the painted walls on the Cour des Voraces.

Unesco registers as part of the World Heritage Sites – whether man-made or natural – the places which have an exceptional and universal value. Lyon is so rich in monuments that it deserved to be part of this prestigious group, numbering 500 sites or world monuments. Twenty-two of them are French for instance, the Mont Saint Michel, the medieval City of Carcassonne, Sainte Madeleine's Abbey in Vezelay or even the Petite France district in Strasbourg. Lyon is therefore sitting pretty among the Machu Pichu in Peru, Prague, Venice or Saint Petersburg.

On December 5th, Lyon's entire historic site was officially accepted as part of the World Heritage by a Unesco Committee which gathered in Kyoto, Japan.

Out went Myrlingue and its foggy skies. As in the tale, the Ugly Duckling turned into a beautiful swan : Lyon, a multi-facetted city of lights and colours, is looked upon as one of the Wonders of the world.

Gallo-roman Lyon

A mosaic from the Gallo-Roman Civilisation Museum.

No one knows precisely when Lugdunum was founded and it has been a controversial issue among historians as the old writers did not leave much information about it. The history of Lugdunum is based essentially on numerous archeological discoveries and on epigraphy.

If Cicero's writings are to be taken for granted, in 44 BC, a rebellion of the inhabitants of Vienna against the Roman veterans of the 5th Legion explains why they were expelled from the town and why they settled at the confluence of the Saône and the Rhône. Those soldiers had been positioned in Vienna by Caesar who wanted to keep an eye on the colony that was hostile to the dictator.

The exchange of letters that occurred between Cicero and Munatius Plancus shows that the latter asked the senate's permission to grant plots of land to the veterans to prevent them from rallying Antony's cause.

Lyon's four aqueducts :
The Mont d'Or aqueduct (10,000 m³ per day),
The Izeron aqueduct (13,000 m³ per day),
The Brévenne aqueduct (66km long, 28,000 m³)
The Gier aqueduct (85 km long, 25,000m³, 1,70 meter wide pipes).

At the Plat-de-l'Air, in Chaponost, 1500 meters of the Gier aqueduct can still be seen.

Hadrien's theater on Fourvière Hill. In the background, the Odeon.

On October 10th, 43, Munatius Plancus traced the *"decumanus maximus"* - today's rue Cleberg, according to Amable Audin – then the *"cardo maximus"*, the two main perpendicular streets, thus defining the limits of the colony that was to be called Lugdunum.

At that time, the Gauls of the Celtic tribe of the Ségusiaves were occupying the region but were scattered in various locations. Condate, the Gaul burrough that had settled in Croix-Rousse Hill would only be populated later, when Fourvière was founded.

The Nautes of the Saône settled on the right side of the river. On the island of Canabaes, at the meeting between the Saône and the Rhône (today's Ainay district) the town's trade was made by merchants and settlers.

Undergoing Celtic and eastern influences, the Roman civilisation lost its founding values. That was why Augustus tried to reorganise the institutions in 27BC, with the creation of the worship to the Emperor. He decided that Lugdunum would be the capital of the three Gauls and entrusted his son-in-law Agrippa with the creation of the road network departing from the city itself.

God Larve. Gallo-Roman Civilisation Museum.

Then he asked Drusus, in 12BC, to build the federal sanctuary of the three Gauls. It was the official and compulsory site of imperial worship and the yearly meeting place of the representatives of the sixty Gaul tribes.

Some thirty odd years later, upon Tibere's request, Rufus, the priest of Rome and of Augustus financed the construction cost of the amphitheater of Croix-Rousse where gladiatorial fights and oratory competitions took place. The city already numbered 50,000 inhabitants.

Emperor Claudius was born in Lugdunum in 10BC. He asked the Senate that the inhabitants of the city be granted Roman citizenship in a very famous speech engraved in the bronze works of the Claudian table.

Between the years 117 and 138 when Emperor Hadrien reign-ed, Lugdunum was at the apex of its glory. The Croix-Rousse amphitheater was extended and could hold 20,000 spectators ;

Mosaic representing a dolphin from Saint-Laurent's Basilica in Choulans. Gallo-Roman Civilisation Museum.

Mosaic representing circus games. Gallo-Roman Civilisation Museum.

the federal sanctuary was also enlarged and two gigantic columns – 14 meters high – were added. A new forum was built on Fourvière Hill as well as the circus and the odeon. Augustus' theater was also extended and could sit 10,000 spectators.

Hadrien started the building of Cybele's sanctuary above Fourvière's theater. On his altar, some terrible rituals took place : floggings, bull sacrifices and castrations. Such rituals were later to be replaced by the martyrdom of Lyonese Christians.

In the middle of the 2nd century, many Christians led by the first bishop, Pothin, settled in Lugdunum. They all believed in a single, loving God and strongly refused to submit to the official worship which they considered as an abominable apostasy.

The martyrs' crypta in the Antiquaille. A 19th century mosaic.

The Three-Gauls Amphitheater on Croix-Rousse Hill.

They were then looked upon as rebellious citizens who could jeopardize the emperor's power. They were wrongfully accused and held responsible for all the disasters. Their atheism was said to irritate the gods and they were treated as the scapegoats of a jumbled society.

In 177, on Good Friday – Easter, that year, took place at the same time as Cybele's celebration – the crowds vented their anger on those innocent people whose tortures were recorded in the Letter of Lyonese Christians to their Asian and Phrygian brothers.

Nineteen were stiffled to death in prison, among whom Pothin ; twenty-four were beheaded because they were Roman citizens and six were fed to beasts among whom Sainte Blandine who tamed the wild beasts who lay down next to her feet.

A few years later, Septimus Severius and Albinus were at odds on account of Lugdunum itself. The power struggle triggered off reprisals, destructions and bootings which all portended the decline of the city. Roman domination was present until 457 when the Burgunds invaded and called it Lugdon.

Close-up on the opus reticulum of a Roman aqueduct and its brick inlay.

tHe "tRaBOuLes"
the covered passageways of Lyon

Certain historic places are absolute time-machines and such is the case for the Traboules of Lyon. When I was still a teenager and I loitered in those narrow streets, I could feel the presence of all the people who had wandered there before me as if the memory of the stones warped time and drew them closer to me.

I expected to chance upon them round the corner of those narrow footpaths that branch off into long corridors and interior courtyards, crossing sometimes more than one building and passing from one street to the next.

The oval staircase of the Maison du Soleil 2, rue Saint-Georges.

The extraordinary cour des Voraces (9, Place Colbert) on the evening of December 8th.

The word "*traboule*" comes from the Latin language : "*trans*" which means to cross and "*ambulare*" which means to move hence the verb, in French, trabouler and the noun, traboule. René Dejean explains that linguist expert André Compan showed that in the Oc language, the words "*travoulo*" or "*traboulo*" mean "*shortcut*". This is so appropriate for Lyons' paths.

Such streets do not only exist in Lyon. They appeared there first in the 4th century on the hills of Croix-Rousse – because of the Canuts who transported all their rolls of silk through those paths – which are as rich in those architectural wonders as in the Presqu'île Peninsula.

The diversity of the traboules is incredible : going from the simple passageway constituted of a long corridor linking two streets together, to the one with different floors as can be found in the Cour des Voraces where it goes down seven floors, crosses an alley and two buildings before exiting two streets below. The maze of traboules is so complex that many inhabitants' lives were saved there either during the French Revolution or during the Second World War.

Traboules with Gothic style intersecting ribs.

Then you will also discover miraboules. The word was made up by Félix Benoit in 1961 because these paths open only on one side and end in an interior courtyard which you can visit to admire (mirar) either the yard or the stairwell.

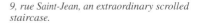

9, rue Saint-Jean, an extraordinary scrolled staircase.

It is believed that there are approximately 400 ancient traboules. As for the beautiful traboules of the left bank, no one has numbered them yet.

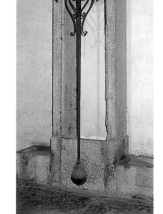

Many traboules were equipped with wells or pumps, such as this one in the Rue Royale.

No one can understand how amazing and architecturally stunning these streets are unless you take a stroll in the maze and peek at this wealth. The list that you find below is far from exhaustive and you can, if you wish, push a door open and catch of glimpse of what is hidden behind. You should always respect the privacy of the people who live there though, because despite the agreement signed between the owners and the tourist office, all are considered private property and deserve to be respected as such.

28, rue Saint-Jean.

The Hôtel Croppet (end of the 15th century), 14, rue du Bœuf.

9, rue Saint-Jean.

The Palais des Laurencins (16th century), 24, rue Saint-Jean..

6, rue des Trois-Maries.

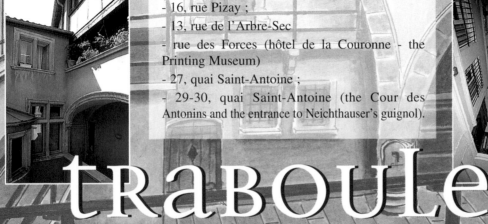

VIEUX-LYON :

- 2, rue Saint-Georges ;
- from 24, rue Saint-Jean to 1, rue du Bœuf (hotel Laurencin) ;
- from 27, rue Saint-Jean to 6, rue des Trois-Maries ;
- 54, rue Saint-Jean ;
- 14, rue du Bœuf ;
- 16, rue du Bœuf (one of the two Rose Towers) ;
- 27, rue du Bœuf ;
- 4, rue Juiverie (Henri IV style house) ;
- 8, rue Juiverie (the Philibert de l'Orme gallery).

CROIX-ROUSSE pentes :

- 19, rue René-Leynaud – Rue Burdeau, the famous Thiaffait passage ;
- 9, place Colbert (the Cour des Voraces) ;
- 2, rue Romarin

PRESQU'îLe :

- 54, rue Mercière
- 58, rue Mercière
- 16, rue Pizay ;
- 13, rue de l'Arbre-Sec
- rue des Forces (hôtel de la Couronne - the Printing Museum)
- 27, quai Saint-Antoine ;
- 29-30, quai Saint-Antoine (the Cour des Antonins and the entrance to Neichthauser's guignol).

The Hôtel de la Couronne, 13, rue de la Poulaillerie.

27, quai Saint-Antoine.

2, rue Romarin.

tRABOULes

the old Lyon district

The oldest district of the town which is like a village within the city can be discovered in three different ways. You can get a general view from Fourvière Hill and you will see it nestling at the bottom of the hill. It is the greatest Renaissance site in France and the second largest in Europe after Venice which has been preserved. From the belvedere, you will be able to catch sight of the multi-coloured Roman tiles and admire the numerous Renaissance towers which majestically dominate the area.

The aldermen's coat of arms decorate the Rue Juiverie.

You can also get a good view from the Saône embankment. In the morning, arriving from the Place Bellecour, you will reach the embankement on the left side and will be spellbound before the ochre and rosy row of façades glimmering in the honey and amber waters of the river.

You can walk your way around the pebbled streets of the district. You cannot discover Lyon from the inside of your car, you must walk around to get the real feel of the city.

In 1964, this district was the first in France to be granted the title of *"preserved area"* by the Malraux Ministry. The association in favour of the *"Renaissance of the Old Lyon"*, at work since the 1950s, played a major

Fifteen Renaissance towers can be found in this part of the Old Lyon district – a view taken from Fourvière Hill.

role in the classification of these districts and opposed their destruction for town planning and public health reasons.

Composed from north to south of the Saint Paul, Saint George, and Saint Jean districts, Old Lyon highlights the magnificence of the town in the 15th and 16th centuries. In 1462, King Louis XI allowed four free fairs to be held. Merchant bankers of all nations flocked to the city and of those the Italians were the primary group who stayed.

At the same time, the King and his court often stayed in Lyon. Silk weaving was promoted by King Louis XI and Francis I. Printing was developed by Barthélemy Buyer and Lyon became its capital. Many artists, scholars and poets could be seen and listened to in the various bookshops and contributed to the cultural enrichment of the period.

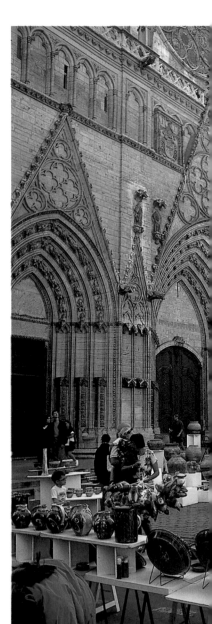

Exhibits of pottery, in front of the Saint-Jean-Baptiste church

These were such thriving times that sumptuous Gothic or Renaissance abodes were built with a lot of character defined today as Lyonese. They look rather plain from the outside but are rather luxurious on the inside. A certain spirit of competition accompanied the building of those magnificent houses as to who would have the most beautiful courtyard, the most original staircase tower or the most elaborate arcade galleries. Hôtel Bullioud (designed by Philibert de l'Orme in 1536) is most definitely the winner with its gallery counterbuttressed by

The Old Lyon district from the Saint-Antoine's embankment.

two penditive turrets. In fact, it is the patent sign of the architectural renaissance of French masons.

All the houses are built the same way, with two different wings parallel to the street and separated by a courtyard where a staircase tower enables people to reach the different floors through the open arcade galleries, or even a belvedere with its vegetable garden and its stable which particularly impressed Rabelais.

Some people still see the influence of the Florentine style in this district. Despite the fact that by the end of the 16th century 2/3 of the foreigners living in Lyon resided next to the Place du Change (Stock Exchange Square), surprisingly they did not influence the style of the houses. Their wealth enabled them to build large and luxurious edifices but they chose to stick to the existing architectural style.

Saint John's Cathedral is the heart of the district and Saint Paul's collegiate church is the oldest religious building. (see the chapter on "*Religious monuments*"). Saint George, built in the neo-Gothic style was constructed in 1844 by Bossan who called it a youthful indiscretion. It is currently the parish used by traditionalist catholics.

Concerning civilian architecture, some edifices should be be mentioned :

The Grand palais des Laurencins - cloth merchants in the Rue St Jean – and its octogonal tower.

Four of the three-hundred-and twenty medallions on the façade of the Cathedral.

On Saint-Jean's square, Saint-John-the Baptist's fountain (1844) presents Jesus' Baptism.

Place du Change.

Maison Mayet in the Flamboyant Gothic style, rue Lainerie.

The Maison des Avocats, Rue de la Bombarde, a.k.a. Cour de la Basoche, is the typical example of successful renovation.

The Maison du Cribble, Rue du Bœuf, is famous for its rose tower.

The Loge du Change (Change Lodge), situated Place du Change, was enlarged in 1747 by Soufflot and aimed at accommodating money changers when fairs took place.

Rue de la Bombarde, the Maison des Avocats.

Opposite the page, the exceptional gallery by Philibert de l'Orme.

The Hôtel Paterin a.k.a Henri IV style house displays three floors of galeries and a superb scrolled straicase.

Place de la Trinité, for example at the bottom of the Gourguillon rise will forever remain famous because of the Punch and Judy show that took place in the Maison du Soleil (the House of the Sun) right across the plazza.

Be on the look out for mullion windows, basket-handle doors, traboules with intersecting rib vaults, spiral staircases or towers, streets or plazzas.

This historic district also has its own museum housed within the spacious Hôtel de Gadagne.

Old Lyon is a lively place where craftsmen like to meet and exhibit their crafts and works of art, every Sunday , at the Saint George Market.

Rue Saint-Jean, Old Lyon's main street.

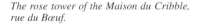

The rose tower of the Maison du Cribble, rue du Bœuf.

Various shop-signs : the cannon, rue de la Bombarde, the bull, rue du bœuf.

Lyon's Pennons Festival reenacts the history of the town.

The Canuts' skills at mastering and recognizing each thread and netting needles.

silk weaving

A s early as the Middle Ages, silk weaving evoked prestige and luxury but silk imports were extremely costly. In 1466, King Louis XI decided that a manufacture would be created fabricating gold sheets and silk ; however, the Lyonese Consulate brought the project to an end because of the influence of the Italian bankers and merchants living in Lyon who traded with Italy.

Francis I wanted to ruin Genoa's economy on account of their support to Charles Quint. In 1515, he grew aware of Lyon's commercial growth – it was the bridgehead of his Italian conquests – and of the trading value of silk in his kingdom. He renewed Charles VIII's order forbidding the use of foreign silk and

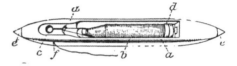

issued a decree in favour of foreign weavers settling in his kingdom and exempting them from tax.

From that moment on, the Consulate's attitude changed. In 1536, two Piedmontese weavers, Etienne Turquet and Barthélemy Nariz were allowed to install mechanical looms in the Saint George district. In 1540, the King issued another order declaring that Lyon was to be « the only repository storing any kind of silk entering the kingdom. »

In 1554, the Union of Workers making a living out of *"gold sheets, silver and silk"* was created for the 12,000 of them working in the silk trade. But the quality of the silk produced was not on a par with the Italian material. In 1606, Lyonese weaver Claude Dangon perfected a loom which enabled at last the long-awaited making of large fashion designed fabrics. In 1667, Colbert, a minister of King Louis XIV, mentored the companies representing French know-how and founded the Grande Fabrique – large manufacture – a trade-union gathering all the silk trade participants and determining quality criterion. Lyon started to have its own original style developed by local draughtsmen.

When Lyon's fame became world-wide, the revocation of the Nantes Edict entailed the exile of

The harmonious and noble alliance of wood and silk.

all the protestant bankers, makers and weavers, reducing their number from 13,000 to 4,000. But the silk trade of the town returned to normal and a new style expanded under the influence of the flower painters, the Gobelins and the Savonnerie. The question was asked : *"Wouldn't it be a good idea, then, to found a drawing school ?"* And it was, in 1756.

Twenty-four draughtsmen worked in Lyon in 1790, the most famous of whom being Philippe de Lasalle who was at the same time an ingenious inventor, weaver, merchant and mechanic. Lyon became the capital of silk and French fashion and later was world-wide renowned.

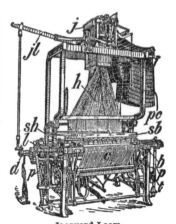

Jacquard Loom.
b, breast-beam; *c*, cloth; *d*, driving-crank; *h*, harness; *j*, Jacquard apparatus; *jl*, Jacquard lever; *l*, lay; *pc*, pattern-cards; *p, p*, picker-sticks; *sb*, swivel-batten; *sh*, shipper-handle; *t*, take-up wheel.

But the Canuts silk workers still lived in miserable conditions and grew increasingly bitter. When they revolted in 1744 and 1786, they only wanted their talents to be recognised but no one paid them any heed. After the French Revolution, feeling swindled, they gave up the fight. Many makers went their own ways and many workshops closed down. Out of 18,000 looms in 1787 only 2,000 were running in 1793.

In 1804, Joseph Marie Jacquard designed, using Vaucanson's work, a new weaving loom which could increase productivity with the use of punch card programming. Because of the size of those new looms, the making of silk was transferred to Croix-Rousse, which thus became *"the Working Hill"*.

The silk workshop of the association "Living Silk" on Croix-Rousse.

In 1831, 6,000 Canuts demonstrated in favour of the minimum wage. The prefect gave them the go-ahead but the merchants refused to pay them and so the fight went on and on. They brandished their black flags and shouted their famous slogan : *"Live to Work or Die Fighting."* The fight continued on with the Voraces who were libertarian social democrats and who also took part in the 1848 Revolution.

Enamelled copper of a weighing-machine used to dry and weigh silk threads.

Despite these uprises, the number of looms kept increasing. There were 60,000 of them in 1848 and the record was even broken in 1853 with a 2,200 ton production of raw silk.

Two years later, the silk worm disease ravaged French breedings. Pasteur worked at finding a remedy but the damage was done and half the production of silk had to be imported. Industrialisation was on its way and

the appearance of synthetic fibers gave silk its finishing stroke. In 1930 the printing technique called "*à la Lyonnaise*" was invented and silk screen printing replaced block printing.

Today all the looms are modernised, computerized and air-jet run, yet only 350 tons of silk are still made in Lyon. A few prestigious workshops produce some hand-made silk to keep the old gestures of the Canut workers alive : in fact, they carry out the orders of the Historic Monuments or of the most famous Haute Couture designers.

The Maison des Canuts, situated in the Rue d'Ivry, has become a museum which re-enacts Lyon's silk weaving trends. If you also visit the Musée des Tissus – the Museum of Fabrics – you will be able to admire centuries of Lyonese silk.

Silk has always been associated with elegance.

George Mattelon, an authentic canut from Croix-Rousse, still shows how a loom functions.

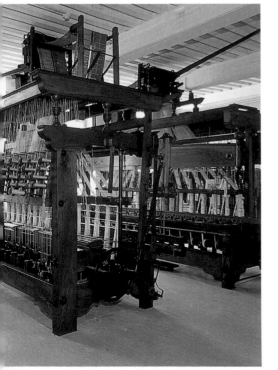

At the Maison des Canuts, Eric is weaving
silk velvet.

At the Maison des Canuts, an authentic
Jacquard loom.

Lyon's signature enhances this silk fabric.

the Religious City

The history of the Lyonese church has been one of the most prestigious in Christendom since the martyrdom of Sainte Blandine, Bishop Pothin and their companions, in the Three Gauls' amphitheater on Croix-Rousse Hill, in the year 177. A great many monuments relate the chronicle of Lyonese Christians and of their astounding worship to the Virgin Mary spanning eighteen centuries. Three hundred and fifty madonnas overlooking many street corners are proof of such devotion. It is reported that Saint Irénée, Lyon's second bishop after Saint Pothin in 177 was the first to speak with the Immaculate Conception.

Rue des Augustins, one of the 300 madonnas, half of which was stolen from the nooks. In 1912, André George presented Lyon as the richest town in statues of the Virgin Mary.

Other examples of this devotion are the foundation of the Hôtel-Dieu (a hospital) in 549 under the protection of the Virgin Mary, the edification of a chapel on Fourvière Hill dedicated to "the blessed Virgin Mary and to Saint Thomas à Becket of Canterbury", and also the creation of the General Alms Charity in 1533 in order to put an end to misery.

This devotion was reinforced by vows.

Saint-Martin and Saint-Loup's abbey on the Island of Barbe (12th century) is the oldest Lyonese monastery founded in the 5th century.

In Saint-Nizier's church, Our Lady of Grace, a masterpiece by Coysevox (1697).

Saint-Nizier's church : the perfect alliance of the Gothic, Renaissance and 19th century styles on the façade.

In the 17th century, the plague devastated the population. The provost of the merchants and the aldermen decided to call on Mary's help. They vowed to erect two statues in Her honour and to walk in procession for Her every year "*... to attend mass, pray to the Virgin and offer her 7 pounds of white wax... and a gold coin... .*"

The plague disappeared completely and September 8th became one of the great religious celebrations in Lyon.

After Napoleon III's defeat in 1870 and upon the request of the Lyonese ladies, Bishop Ginoulhiac solemnly promised to build a sanctuary on Fourvière Hill – greatly approved of by many inhabitants – if the Prussians did not invade Lyon. His wish was granted : the Prussians settled in Dijon and did not march on to Lyon despite the order they had received.

Architect Pierre Bossan supervised the building of the chapel in 1872, and it was consecrated in 1896 by Cardinal Couillé. Bossan was influenced by the mystical Lyonese school owned by the painter Louis Janmot, and therefore viewed the sanctuary on Fourvière as "*the palace of the*

Saint-Jean's episcopal garden contains the vestiges of two churches and of a 4th century baptistery.

most powerful of queens...", the "*Turris davidica*" of the Virgin Mary's litanies.

The neobyzantine decoration composed of sculptures, gildings and colours is devoted to Mary's life and is a reminder of the place she holds within France's history and the world.

Among the 56 churches of Lyon, several are worth mentioning. Saint Martin-d'Ainay is the oldest church in Lyon and the only one built in Romanesque style since the destruction of the Island of Barbe's abbey whose tympanum has been built into the façade wall. The original decor and the porch-like spire are some of the most interesting elements of the façade.

Inside, the four pillars that surround the transept were taken from the altar to Rome and to Augustus erected on Croix-Rousse Hill in the beginning of the Christian era. In the semicircular cupola vault of the choir, Hippolyte Flandrin painted Christ blessing the Virgin Mary, Blandine, Clothilde and Pothin on a golden mosaic backdrop.

The Romanesque sculpture of the cornices and of the chancel compete with those of some of the most famous churches. On 13 June 1905, Pope Pius X decided to grant this church the status of minor basilica at a time when the conflict between State and Church was raging.

Saint John the Baptist's primatial church was erected in the 12th century in replacement of three churches whose vestiges can be seen in the archeological garden nearby.

Begun in Romanesque style, construction continued through the Gothic period and finally ended in Gothic (type II). The evolution of the different styles is easily noticeable on the triforium.

Among the elements worth noticing on the 17th century façade, are the rose formed by six trefoil circles set in a six petal flower, and the 320 sculpted medallions. 200 of these medallions were unfortunately destroyed by protestants in 1562 together with 50 statues. The astronomical clock from the 16th and 17th centuries still chimes on the hour four times a day.

Saint-Jean's singing school (11th or 12th century) contains the treasure of the cathedral.

Next to it, the Romanesque façade of the Cathedral's singing school (12th century) inspires admiration. It contains the treasure of the Cathedral.

Two assemblies took place in the Cathedral, as well as the wedding of King Henri IV with Marie de Medicis on 13 December 1600.

Saint Nizier's church was built in the 15th century where Saint Pothin had founded his first Christian community. Apart from its two dissimilar steeples, (one from the 15th century and the other from the19th century), an odd-looking ceilinged clock dating back to 1549 decorates the vault of the nave. The statue of Our Lady of Grace sculpted by Coysevox in 1674 and so dear to the Lyonese people, has been placed in that church as well.

The former chapel of the Chartreuse du Lys, also known as Saint Bruno's church on Croix-Rousse Hill, is a work of art from the Baroque style. The baldaquin of the chancel

In Saint-Bruno's church, the magnificent baroque baldaquin and altar by Servandoni (1738).

Rue Paul-Chenavard, the romanesque porch (12th century) of the former Saint-Pierre's church now part of the Palace of Fine Arts.

The western façade of the basilica at sunset.

surmounted by a magnificent canopy was designed by the Italian artist, Servandoni.

Saint Paul's church mixes Roman and Gothic styles. Several remarkable sections date back to the 12th century : Saint Laurent's door, the projecting ornaments around the roof edges and the hexagonal cupola decorated with a two-tier blind arcade. Others date back to the 15th and the 17th centuries, especially a chapel with its Gothic arch curve, ornamented with medallions featuring choirs of angels.

The neobyzantine gildings of the basilica of Fourvière Hill, devoted to Mary's glory.

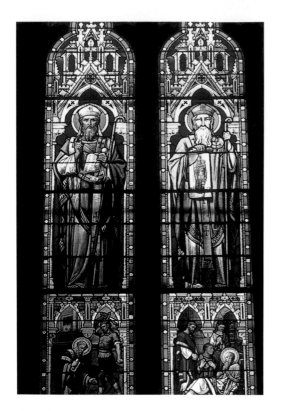

Opposite the church, the statue designed by Jean Charlier evokes the well-known theologian who supported Joan of Arc. He was chancellor at the Université de Paris and became Saint Paul's canon, dedicating his life to the education of the young.

Next to Saint Irénée's church and its crypt to the martyrs, Saint Irénée's Calvary is the last one that dominates the city.

Dating back to the early days of Christianity, the Lyonese mass is one of the great rituals of Christendom. When Pope Pius V permanently codified the Roman ritual, he kept the former rituals that had been used 200 years earlier.

Several Lyonese people spread the faith.

Charles Démia founded the first school for poor children in 1699.

Pauline Jaricot (1799 – 1862) was the founder of the movement for the propagation of the faith and the workers'actions. Her living rosary numbered some two million members throughout the world.

Stained glass window by Lucien Bégule, in Saint-Paul's church, portraying saint Pothin and saint Irénée.

In front of Saint-Paul's, the statue of Gerson, a theologian.

Claudine Thévenet (1775-1836), founder of the Jesus-Mary congregation and the Providence Institution, took care of abandonned girls. She was canonized in 1993.

Frédéric Ozanam created Saint Vincent de Paul's conferences, and Father Chevrier founded the Prado Institution to help workmen in 1864. He was one of the renowned, socially-conscious catholics together with Bishop de Bonald, a founder of workers' associations. By the end of the century, their work resulted in the creation of Christian trade-unions for workers.

Behind Saint-Irénée's church, the last calvary in Lyon, erected in 1814.

As for Bishop de Marion Brésillac, he launched the African Missions in 1856. Finally, Cardinal Gerlier, the archbishop of Lyon during the second World War, stood up to the Nazis and saved a great many Jews and members of the French Resistance.

Among the works of art of Saint-Martin-d'Ainay's abbey, one romanesque capital.

Saint-Martin-d'Ainay's steeple is decorated with small pyramids, brick inlay and a freize with an engraved motif.

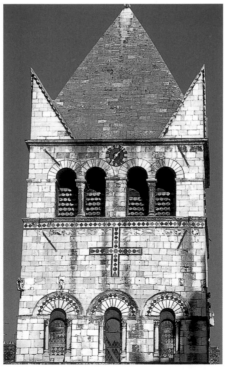

December 8th.

Fabisch's golden Virgin, 5,6 metres tall, overlooking Fourvière.

Opposite : Simon Maupin's town-hall illuminated on the evening of December 8th. Produced by the city of Lyon. Artists : Art et Technique Warrener.

After many long prayers from the aldermen in 1643, for the plague to disappear, their wishes were finally fulfilled and the 8th of September became a Lyonese celebration. The date was chosen in 1852 to bless and inaugurate the large bronze gilded statue of the Virgin Mary placed on the dome of the new steeple, which dominates the city. The statue, which is 5,6-meters high, was designed by Fabisch who would also sculpt the statue of the Miraculous Virgin Mary that can be seen in Lourdes. Unfortunately, the workshop where the statue was kept was flooded by the Saône river, thus postponing the ceremony until December 8th.

That day, the weather was dreadful despite the general good cheer. The bells ringing and the canons booming could be heard all around. Cardinal de Bonald blessed the gilded statue, and at that moment, a terrible storm broke out forcing the crowds to seek shelter. The ceremony was over then and there and the bonfire cancelled.

A few hours later, the wind and rain stopped. The people, deprived of their celebration, came back into the streets and started lighting fires to light up the chapel on Fourvière Hill and the statue. Millions of candles were placed on the window sills of all the city's façades. People celebrated all through the night and the lighting feast of December 8th was born.

The blue and white colours of Fourvière Hill, in the honour of the Virgin Mary.

Two years later, on 8 December 1854, Pope Pius IX proclaimed the dogma of the Immaculate Conception. That day, many Lyonese felt their faith strengthened by the belief that God had chosen Lyon to pay homage to His saintly mother.

The feast of Lights, created to replace the celebration of December 8th has lost all religious connotation. Only a few fervent catholics still walk in procession through the garden of the Rosary perhaps praying for another wish to be granted that would bring the faithful back to Fourvière Hill.

At the end of the' 80s, the municipality of Lyon grew aware of the incredible trump card that these lights represented and how they emphasized the Lyonese monuments with adapted lighting. Working on a project entitled *"Lyon, the City of Lights"*, the town council wanted to prove that the use of these public lights could enrich the city from an aesthetic dimension. In the year 1999, more than 267 monuments were illuminated and transformed each night, and even more so on December 8th. For the 10th anniversary commemorating the Project of Lights, in December 1999, the lighting was exceptional. That night, Lyon was really the *"City of Lights"*. Baudelaire had named it *"City of Coal"*, but, today the town is proud of its title and it exports its savoir-faire throughout the entire world (Saint Petersburg, Havana, Ho Chi Minh City).

Place des Terreaux.
Artists : Christian Gimat, Anne Deporte, Pierre Combescot, Patrice Richard, David Puyoou.
Production : Ad Lib Créations (december 2001).

the monuments

Three of the eight muses of the Opera.

*W*hen Lyon became a World Heritage Site, Unesco experts stressed the readability of historic epochs across the city's monuments. The monuments can be classified chronologically, leaving aside those of Roman or religious import which have been dealt with at length in other chapters.

The 375 meters of the neo-classical façade of the hospital (18th century) and the splendid dome by J.G. Soufflot. Burned down in 1944, it was entirely rebuilt out of concrete according to Soufflot's plans. Rabelais (1532 to 1535) and Nostradamus (1564) were doctors there.

from the 12th to the 17th century

Construction of the Hôtel-Dieu began in the 12th century. It was intended to extend the pre-existing hospital constructed in 549 by the bishop Saint Sacerdos, upon the request of King Childebert of the Burgonds and Queen Ultrogoth, to provide free medical care for pregnant women without resources and the needy.

Thus the Lyonese tradition of charity was born, served as model and was even reinforced in 1665 with the creation of the Community of the Sisters of Charity.

After the French Revolution, the town council joined the Hôtel-Dieu and the hospital of Charity founded by the General Alms, in 1617, thus forming Lyon's public hospital.

The back of the town-hall, on the evening of December 8th.

The large Bellecour Square and its chestnut-trees which will soon be replaced by lime-trees.

In the middle of the square, the new equestrian statue of Louis XIV sculpted by Lemot in 1826.

from the 17th to the 18th century

Construction of Simon Maupin's town-hall started in 1646 in pure Louis XIII's style. It was partly destroyed by fire on 13 September 1672, but Jules-Hardouin Mansart, Louis XIV's architect, restored it in 1699.

Some sights are worth mentioning :

The equestrian statue of Henri IV was designed by sculptor Legendre-Héral in 1827.

The belfry shelters : a sixty-five bell carillon and the 1914 clock which chimes the hours on a 2.1 ton bell and repeats them on another bell weighing 4.3 tons.

The famous *"gold ball"*, often mistaken for a barometer, is in fact an astronomical clock made in 1652 and serves as an astrolab indicating the different phases of the moon.

The three-eyed cyclopse designed by sculptor Lucien Pascal in 1883.

The main stairway is entirely painted and relates an allegory by Thomas Blanchet.

The Palais Saint Pierre situated on Place des Terreaux (the Terreaux Square) is a fine example of the Italian Baroque style. It used to be the convent of the Canonness Ladies of Saint Pierre and today, it hosts the Museum of Fine Arts of Lyon which displays some of the greatest collections of French works with French, Spanish, Flemish, Italian and Dutch paintings but also some of the works from the 19th century Lyonese school. Devastated by the Huguenots in 1562, the abbey was rebuilt in 1686 according to the plans of architect Royer de la Valnefière.

Following a large renovation program, the museum presents paintings, sculptures, Egyptian, Greek and Roman antiquities, and an important

collection of decorative art in a vast number of rooms stretching on a 14,500 meter square surface. It is so rich in works of art that it is the largest museum in France after the Louvre in Paris.

The temple of the Reformed Church (Loge du Change) evokes the role played by the merchant bankers living in the Old Lyon district since the 16th century. As the 17th century construction turned out to be too small, it was enlarged by Soufflot in 1748.

The Superior School of Music of Lyon is situated on the Quai Chauveau in the former buildings of the veterinary school of Bourgelas. It was the former convent of the Sisters of Saint Elisabeth (18th century) and still possesses the cloister and the refectory frescoes.

the 19th century

In 1595, Pré Bellecourt became a square upon Henri IV's request. Louis XIV enlarged it and a statue of the King designed by Desjardins was placed there in 1713 together with the statues of the Coustou brothers representing the Saône and Rhône rivers. Bonarparte later restored them after the damage they had endured during the Convention.

Situated in Place de la Comédie, the Grand Theater of Germain Soufflot was opened in 1756.

The Loge du Change, used today by the Reformed Church as a temple.

The "toaster" of the Opera.

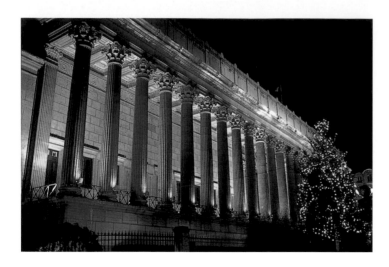

The Law Courts and its 24 pillars, 28 in all including those in the entrance.

Opposite the page : the Celestins' Theater all lit-up on December 8th, 1999. Production : City of Lyon. Artists : Art et Technique Warrener.

The Palais du Commerce designed by architect Dardel (1860)

Inside, the architecture was rather modern for the times, with an oval-shaped room and three retreating galleries. From 1827 to 1831, architects Pollet and Chenavard gave it the character as we knew until 1997 when it was transformed by architect Jean Nouvel and was given a metallic dome, which the Lyonese nicknamed "*Toaster*".

The Celestins' theater was built on the former Celestins' convent in 1407. It was rebuilt in 1877 by Lyonese architect Gaspard André and is one of the last Italian-type theaters in France.

Laid out like a horseshoe around the room, the tiered galleries can be reached through a large atrium decorated with antique masks. The precious decoration and the red and gold colours highlight the spirit at the end of the 19th century. Two hundred and fifty thousand spectators flock there each year to attend the semi-classic, semi-innovative programme chosen by Director Jean-Paul Lucet.

The Palais de Justice (the Law Court) was built in 1835, where the former prison of Roanne had once stood. It was nicknamed "*24 pillars*" and was designed by Louis-Pierre Baltard who found his inspiration in the Greco-Roman style, in vogue at the time. The façade, composed of 24 Corynthian columns defines a long disproportionate peristyle which dominates the entire building. The edifice was heavily criticized at the time. Today, it is used as the Court of Appeal and Assize Court.

The Palais du Commerce (the Trading Palace) which was built in 1860, groups the sections of the Chamber of Commerce and Industry of Lyon. One of the most remarkable features is the stock broker's central enclosure of the former stock exchange. The painted ceiling, supported by caryatids, displays a magnificent allegory.

The Préfecture (Governor's house) and the Conseil Général du Rhône (General Council) were

The former Brotteaux train-station which is now used as an auction-room and a restaurant.

built in 1890 by architect Antonin Louvier. The staircase is monumental and many salons store numerous works of art. The Debate room receives much light through the glass roof designed by Lucien Bégule.

The Tony Garnier Market, which used to be the slaughter-house of the Mouche, is the largest covered surface in Europe. No posts were used to support the weight of the roof which rests on metallic beams erected on ball and socket joints, 120 meters high. Seating capacity is 18,000.

Tony Garnier, an architect with a vision, winner of the Grand Prix de Rome, has designed other buildings in Lyon such as the Grange-Blanche Hospital, the Stadium of Gerland, and his Ideal City partially built in the American district.

The magnificent Tony Garnier covered market.

**« ...267 sites
and monuments
illuminated
each night...»**

The Maurice Ravel Auditorium.

tHe 20tH cENtURY

Errors of judgement made in the 1960s resulted in the building of the Cour de Verdun (which will be demolished in 2006), and the rapid construction of the Part-Dieu district whose aim was to create a second city-center because the Presqu'île Peninsula was over-populated. The *"Pen"* (the Crédit Lyonnais 170 meter tower) sticks out a mile ; the public library is a kind of silo supposed to store two million books ; the auditorium for Lyon's national orchestra is a room the size of its talent ; not to mention the modern TGV train station.

At the end of 20th century, the point was to create quality areas such as the Place des Terreaux or the Cité Internationale designed by architect Renzo Piano, built on the former site of the Fair. The Conference Hall, a cinema, a Hilton hotel and the Museum of Modern Art can be found there, next to Interpol Headquarters.

Mr Raymond Barre, Lyon's mayor, who supports a wide range of projects, is bent on making Lyon one of the leading cities of the Third Millenium.

Next to Interpol Headquarters, the Cité Internationale by architect Renzo Piano contains the Conference Hall, the Museum of Modern Art, a first-class hotel, a movie theater and a casino.

GUIGNOL

Gilbert Pavaly sculpting and painting Guignol's face in his workshop on the Place du Change.

Laurent Mourguet, the son of Canut workers and the creator of Guignol was born in Lyon in 1769. When he was a very young man, he learned the weaving trade.

Around 1797, he became a professional tooth-puller and to respect job rules and attract customers, he put up a little puppet show presenting Italian theater classics. As he felt more drawn to the theater than to the art of dentistry, he created his own little theater where parts of the show were based on improvisations dealing with current events. He would never let go of this habit which would later enable Guignol to display his satirical and irreverent wit.

He started working with a popular comedian called Lambert Grégoire Ladré, a.k.a. Father Thomas, who played deftly on words and bantered away and as a consequence, they struck up a friendship. Both knew that they would only be successful if they resorted to something other than Italian puppets. Their friendship was short-lived, however, because Father Thomas was accustomed to flying into a temper. To replace him, Mourguet created a jolly puppet with a glib tongue, which he called Gnafron. It got its name from a Lyonese word *"gnaffre"* which means shoemaker. Gnafron was a rather colourful character, dressed in a leather apron, and a top hat, red in the face and with a puffy nose.

As Mourguet did not have enough customers, he also worked at the Crèche Brunet, a theater with marionettes pulled by strings. There, he discovered the essence of puppet shows, as he played the role of Father

Guignol from the Guignol Theater, rue Louis Carrant.

47

Coquart, a no-nonsense, popular, happy-go-lucky character who would later inspire the creation of Guignol.

In 1808, he sculpted a puppet to whom he gave his own round face, two mischievous eyes and a funny little turned up nose. He dressed him like Father Coquart, and like the Canut workers of his day and age, i.e. in a brown jacket adorned with golden buttons and a red bow-tie. On his head, he put a soft leather hat with turned down ear-flaps on his "*sarsifis*", which means a braid of hair tied with a ribbon.

Why did he call him Guignol? More than two centuries after his creation, no one knows the answer and we found more than ten different explanations but refuse to let one prevail over the other.

Mourguet then created other characters and acquired a certain fame with the performances he gave of Guignol in his most defined version, in the Café-Théâtre : a satirical puppet, stimulating its own wit to mock his fellow-countrymen's failings. But beyond comedy, with his rather simple morals and his bantering habits, Guignol denounced injustice and was the spokesman of the poor and the needy. With his stick, called « tavelle », a clarinet to make bears dance or American root, Guignol loved justice. As Louis Jacquemin once wrote : "*He fooled the rich and the mighty, beat Policemen, scoffed at the landlord, the sollicitor and even the judge to get away from them all the quicker...*" Such is the spirit of Guignol, and this explains why, two centuries later, we still like him so much.

Guignol making a mockery. Historic Museum of Lyon.

Laurent Mourguet, the toothpuller. Museum Disagn Cardelli, rue Saint-Jean.

Théâtre de Guignol

In Guignol's theater, rue Carrant, some of the collection of puppets and a performance of the "Jam Jar", one of the classical plays.

gastronomy

Right hand page : a great deal of the verve of Lyon's cooking is borrowed from Guignol.

The authentic Lyonese bouchon plaque on the shop front of the Garet.

Maurice Edmond Sailland, a.k.a. Curnonsky, established Lyon as the world capital of gastronomy : *"it deserves that name"*, he said, *"because here, cooking reaches the apex in art, that is to say : simplicity."* In Lyon, indeed, cooking is an art and a chef is more a philosopher than a technician and for him, eating is similar to worshipping a god.

Lyon's inhabitants are so fond of good food that the saying goes in the Presqu'île Peninsula, *"that to seduce a woman, it is wiser to take her to the restaurant than to take her dancing or to a movie."* After all, Lyon is right in the middle of the land of plenty where any kind of product can be found. This abundance of foods gave birth to all kinds of Lyonese specialties, be it the Mères – mothers –, the bouchons – popular little restaurants – or a multitude of rituals and products.

Lyonese Mothers are part of the 19th century legacy. After the French revolution, the cooks of the great bourgeois houses were encouraged, by their masters, to create their own recipes and write them down in copybooks. Some of them, taking advantage of their own skills, opened their restaurants. Others, like Eugénie Brazier, were awarded the three stars of the prestigious Michelin guide. One of her apprentices was Paul Bocuse in 1946. All those Mothers have trained today's great chefs, and their cuisine placed Lyon and France as the leader in the art of eating.

The type of popular restaurant that should be tried in Lyon is called « bouchon », a word created in the 19th century and which comes from Ancient Greece. These restaurants aim at preserving Lyonese cooking traditions. There, you will eat what the Mothers and the Canuts cooked. In a traditional bouchon, all the salad bowls will be placed on the table at the same time ; this table will be covered with a red and white checked tablecloth, the chef will be a diamond in the rough, and the spirit of Lyon mixed with a pinch of Rabelasian wit will be felt more strongly there than anywhere else.

To preserve these traditions, an association has been formed numbering some twenty authentic Bouchons easily recognisable thanks to a plaque featuring Gnafron located on the façade of their restaurant.

A *"mâchon"* is a typically Lyonese meal. According to Félix Benoît : *"A mâchon is not any kind of meal. It is*

In a bouchon, all the salad-bowls are placed on the table at the same time. "Chez Hugon" rue Pizay.

some sort of snack that can be taken either around 9a.m. to pass the morning, or around 5p.m. to avoid starvation until dinner time." It is composed of hot pork meats such as pork rinds but also of various kinds of *"saucisson"*, of *"grattons"* which are made from what is left over from lard and sometimes, salads where you will find mutton foot (clapotons), donkey snout (pieds de moutons), dandelions and giblets, (béatilles).

Since the Gauls, Lyon's specialty is its delicatessen meats (charcuterie) among which you will find the famous *"saucisson de Lyon"* but be careful, it can only be called thus if it contains a 100% pork meat. Another of its characteristic is that the fat has been minced. Rumour had it wrong that it also contained donkey meat. As Gérald Gambier said : *"There's no more donkey meat in the "saucisson de Lyon" than there is lion meat."*

The three musketeers of Lyonese charcuterie are : the Rosette, the Jésus, and the Cervelas, three various types of saucisson or sausage. The latter is for cooking just like the Sabodet which is composed of pork snout and rind.

The famous grattons.

Concerning tripes, the "*andouillette*" is considered Lyonese only if it is mainly composed of crow of veal (fraise de veau) stuffed in veal skin. Various types of tripes called "*gras-double*" and "*tablier de sapeur*" come from a specific part of the veal's stomach called "*bonnet de veau*".

Quenelles are also part of the cuisine, and you know they are cooked to perfection if they melt in you mouth. The secret is the balanced proportion of ingredients ; 1/3 pike, 1/3 fat, 1/3 bread soup.

There are two Lyonese cheeses which are well-renowned : "*fromage fort*" which means strong cheese and the "*cervelle de canut*" which means Canut's brain. "*Fromage fort*" really deserves its name as various old cheeses are mixed with white wine in an earthenware salad bowl.

As for sweets and desserts, Lyon invented the "*bugnes*", a sort of doughnut, and the "*papillottes*", a sort of chocolate candy.

Thus, the former capital of the Three Gauls stands out in terms of gastronomy and so it is not surprising that Lyonese chef Paul Bocuse should be the ambassador of French cuisine in the world.

Colette Sibilla, the queen of the Part-Dieu covered market.

At the "Petit Bouchon Chez Georges", a truly warm and hospitable restaurant.

THE CERVELLE DE CANUTS,
(after a recipe
from the nineteenth century.)

For 2: take two well drained soft cheeses. Beat them well to obtain a very creamy texture. Add a splash of vinegar, 10cl of roasted soy oil, 1 big sliced shallot, 15g of chopped chives, 5cl dry white wine, salt and pepper to taste and a good spoonful of crème fraîche. If you like it (and if you have no romantic date that evening), you can add a small amount of crushed garlic. Then again, you might be eating it together... Beat the mixture well before pouring it into the serving dish, sprinkling parsley and chives. Serve very cold with a good Beaujolais.

"Papillottes, coussins and cocons", three typical Lyonese specialties.

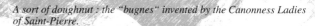

A sort of doughnut : the "bugnes" invented by the Canonness Ladies of Saint-Pierre.

(1) : From *The traditions of Lyon's gastronomy* by G. Gambier, same editor.

the painted walls

Tony Garnier Urban Museum (detail).

W̱all painting is part of the world's history and Lyon is no exception to the rule. On Fourvière Hill, traces of painted walls can still be seen amidst the Roman ruins. Several churches have kept the remaining marks of old frescoes on their walls. From 1662 to 1675, Thomas Blanchet, *"an everyday painter of the city of Lyon"*, decorated the entire town-hall with mythological allegories.

The 19th century was the most productive of all. The Lyonese school of painting was particularly well-known at the time, notably in religion, and benefitted from orders due to the prosperity of the silk production. Lyon then became known as the town of the Pre-Raphaelite style, because of artists like Louis Janmot (Saint-Polycarpe's or Saint-Francis-de-Salles's churches) and Hippolyte Flandrin (who designed Saint-Martin-d'Ainay's apse).

The stairway of Saint-Pierre's palace is decorated with the portrait of Pierre Puvis de Chavannes, the master of Symbolism.

In the Conseil Général building, Louis-Edouard Fournier painted an immense fresco as a tribute to the Lyonese Glory and Beaujolais Wine.

Thomas Blanchet, main staircase, in the town-hall.

Pierre Puvis de Chavanne, Christian Inspiration, in the staircase of the Museum of Fine Arts.

The American district.
In April 1991, Unesco gave the museum the title of "World Decade of Cultural Development".
Designed by Cité de la Création.

In the 20th century, three other churches were decorated : Saint-Paul's by Paul Borel, Saint-Jacques-le-Majeur's by Louise Cottin and Saint-Pierre-de-Vaise by Claudius Barriot. But inside public edifices, the ornamentation was grandiose. At the Hôtel des Postes (Post Office Hotel), a 54-meter wall painting painted by Louis Bouquet in 1937 evokes Lyon and its radiance. The façade of the Stock Exchange was decorated with an immense mosaic made by F. Fargeot in 1934.

Over the last twenty years, more than 150 walls have been painted by painters who wished to present a public and popular view of art. This new style of wall-painting, often in trompe-l'œil style, has been encouraged by the public and by organisations like Unesco which awarded the Tony Garnier Urban Museum the label of "*World Decade of Cultural Development*", in 1991.

Thanks to the teams of painters such as Cité de la Création, Mur'Art or even freelance wall painters, Lyon can be regarded today as the French capital of wall painting and more and more tourists flock to the city to admire them, each year.

Some of these wall-paintings are absolute "musts".

Ideal Mexican City. *Tony Garnier Urban Museum, by Cité de la Création.*

The Library of the City, *viewed by Cité de la Création.*

The Canuts' wall-painting, which is the largest trompe-l'œil in Europe with its 1,200 m², is the memory-wall of Croix-Rousse Hill (painted by Cité de la Création.)

At the bottom of Croix-Rousse Hill, 30 famous characters from the capital of the Gauls cover the entire wall on the fresco of the Lyonese people. (Cité de la Création).

In Vaise, the Comics boulevard, Rue Marietton is composed of five painted walls based on the works of contemporary draughtsmen. (Mur'Art).

The Urbain Tony Museum exhibits 25 frescoes on a total surface of 5,500 meter square area, all referring to the theme of Tony Garnier's ideal city and using the works of six contemporary foreign artists. (Cité de la Création).

The Silk Door – porte de Soie – is part of the program entitled *"the Streets of Silk throughout Lyon's Croix-Rousse Hill"* approved of by Unesco. It evokes 3,000 years of silk history. (Cité de la création).

The enclosing wall of the C.R.I.R. portrays 165 athletes on a 500 meter-long fresco running along the beltway. (Vincent Ducaroy and Mireille Perrin).

Vaise, the boulevard de la B.D., *by Mur'Art : based on a drawing by Jacques de Loustal.*

In the Old Lyon district, the wall of the Cour des Loges, *by Mur'Art.*

The Wall of the Canuts, *repainted in 2002.*
Designed by Cité de la Création.

The Fresco of the Lyonese people. *Designed by Cité de la Création.*

Lyon, City of light. Half-millennium mural. Saint-Jean-de-Dieu Hospital, 8th arrondissement. Created by Georges Faure and his group *Les Éléphants Heureux (The happy Elephants).*

The impossible marathon. *Designed by Vincent Ducaroy et Mireille Perrin.*

(1) See Murs Peints de Lyon d'hier et d'aujourd'hui
by Gérald Gambier, same editor.

parks and museums

In the Parc de la Cerisaie, on Croix-Rousse Hill, apart from the Villa Gillet, 300 vine plants are labelled with the names of famous people. Croix-Rousse wine of is a rival to Montmartre wine.

Lyon is sometimes known as a city in the countryside with its 20,000 tall trees lining the streets and parks and its vegetable growers whose plots of land lie one kilometer away from the Montée des Soldats – Soldiers' Hill.

Lyon aims at improving its green spaces and has, for that purpose, launched a project entitled *"nature in Lyon"*. It is essentially based on eliminating the trees which are too old or sick and on embellishing the city with new trees and plants or forgotten species.

This project concerns many parks and gardens.

The terrasses of Perrache are immense suspended gardens built in 1976, above Perrache's exchange center. You can get a really nice view of Lyon from up there.

The Chartreux garden, which was presumably created by the Bülher brothers in 1855, is 10,626 m² wide and looks like a cascade of terrasses flowing down the hill that links the Saône embankment with the Croix-Rousse plateau. From there, you can get a splendid view of the Saône river and Fourvière Hill.

A Spanish mason's secret garden nestles at 83, Grande rue on Croix-Rousse Hill. His name was Jules Senis-Mir and he wanted to recreate a sort of Lyonese Alhambra for his mother.

The beautiful garden of Rosa Mir.

The Parc de la Tête d'Or – the Golden Head Park – was called thus because it is said that a treasure and a gold head representing Christ's face were found there. It was designed by the Bülher brothers and covers a surface of 260 acres. It is also famous for its magnificent rose garden in which 60,000 rose-bushes bloom each year and are photographed by many tourists.

Sportsmen and walkers love to jog or loiter there because it is a refreshing place to be in and pollution free. The botanical garden presents 3,500 species of worldwide plants on its 18 acres or in its 5,000 m2 of green-houses. The zoo has 250 mammals, 400 birds and 80 reptiles.

Between the museum parks and the museums themselves, it is just a hop, skip and jump away.

A renovated room and the garden of the Saint-Pierre Museum.

The garden of the Saint-Pierre Museum (the Museum of Fine Arts) is for the Lyonese people a haven of peace. It was arranged within the former cloister of the convent of the Ladies of Saint-Pierre and stores Parthenon friezes as well as mosaics and bronze sculptures by Carpeau, Rodin, Bourdelle, etc.

Situated within the archeological park of Fourvière Hill, the Museum of Gallo-Roman Civilisation displays the most varied archeological collections in

France just after those of the National Museum in Paris. The museum recreates four centuries of life, customs, beliefs, arts and institutions in Lugdunum from the remains and objets found for the most part in Lyonese soil.

The Museum of Textiles, situated within the Hôtel de Villeroy enables visitors to follow the evolution of weaving and interior design through Eastern and Western materials. A large importance is given to Lyonese silk. The Museum of Decorative Arts completes the Museum of Textiles as it shows the use of fabric and tapestries in the 17th and 18th centuries of interior design.

One of the rooms of the sumptuous museum of Fabrics and Decorative Arts, an absolute must.

The Museum of Natural History is the largest museum in France after the one in Paris and offers a journey through the history of nature by focusing on zoology, geology, ethnography and ecology. Two rooms dedicated to the Egyptian and oriental arts complete the tour.

The Museum of Firefighters displays a wide variety of fire pumps from the 17th century to today, various apparatus, a fine collection of helmets and an impressive collection of vehicles.

The Parc de la Tête d'Or : a lovely and refreshing place in the middle of the city.

The Museum of Printing and Banking retraces the history of printing and of the diverse techniques used over the centuries with a particular emphasis on Lyonese printing which reached its apex in the 16th century.

The Historic Museum of Lyon evokes Lyon's history from the Middle Ages to the 20th century through archeological collections, china, pieces of furniture and works of art. One section of the museum is the International Museum of Puppets. This making perfect sense as Lyon is Guignol's hometown.

The museum on Fourvière Hill is dedicated to Sacred Art. Many collections of jewellery, religious clothing, ex-votos and works about the building of the basilica can be seen there.

Finally, the Museum of Civil Hospices is situated inside the Hôtel-Dieu and two apothecaries can be visited there. The museum presents Lyonese medical life through many objects and works of art.

Inside the beautiful Hôtel de Gadagne: Lyon's Historic Museum and the Puppet Museum.

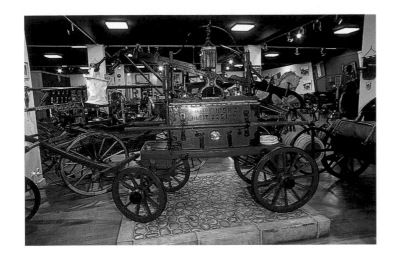

At la Duchère, the Firefighters Museum.

At the Civil Hospital Museum, the Charity Apothecary.

BIBLIOGRAPHY

Audin (Amable), *Lyon miroir de Rome*, Librairie Arthème Fayard, Paris, 1989 ;
Boucher (Jacqueline), *Présence Italienne à Lyon à la Renaissance, du milieu du XVe à la fin du XVIe siècle*, L.U.G.D., Lyon, S.D. ;
Bouzard (Marie), *La Soierie Lyonnaise du XVIIIe au XXe siècle*, Ed Lyonnaises d'Art et d'Histoire, Lyon, 1997 ;
Dejean (René), *Traboules de Lyon, histoire secrète d'une ville*, Editions Le Progrès, Lyon, 1988 ;
Gambier (Gérald), *Les Traditions de la cuisine Lyonnaise*, Editions La Taillanderie, Châtillon-sur-Chalaronne, 2002 ;
Gambier (Gérald), *Murs peints de Lyon, d'hier et d'aujourd'hui*, Editions La Taillanderie, Châtillon-sur-Chalaronne, 2002 ;
Gouttard (Marie), *Les Madones de Lyon*, Editions La Taillanderie, Bourg-en-Bresse, 1991 ;
Jacquemin (Louis), *Guide de Lyon et la Courly*, Editions La Taillanderie, Bourg-en-Bresse, 1989 ;
Jacquemin (Louis), *Le Vieux-Lyon*, Editions La Taillanderie, Bourg-en-Bresse, 1995 ;
Jacquemin (Louis), *Histoire des églises de Lyon*, Vaulx-en-Velin, Bron, Vénissieux, Saint-Fons, Ed. Elie Bellier, Lyon, 1985 ;
Jacquemin (Louis), *Lyon palais et édifices publics*, Editions La Taillanderie, Attignat, 1987 ;
Jacquemin (Louis), *Traboules et Miraboules*, Editions La Taillanderie, Châtillon-sur-Chalaronne, 1999 ;
Mérindol (Pierre), *Lyon, les passerelles du temps,* Editions La Taillanderie, Bourg-en-Bresse, 1988 ;
Mesplède (Jean-François), *Saveurs de Lyon et du Rhône*, Ed. La Taillanderie, Bourg-en-Bresse, 1996 ;
Neyret (Régis), *Guide historique de Lyon*, Ed du Tricorne, Genève, Ed Lyonnaises d'Art et d'Histoire, Lyon, 1998 ;
Nicolas (Marie-Antoinette), *Le Vieux-Lyon, Old Lyons, 5 circuits*, Edition Lyonnaise d'Art et d'Histoire, Lyon, 1995 ;
Pelletier (André) et Rossiaud (Jacques), *Histoire de Lyon, Antiquité et Moyen Age*, Ed. Horvath, Le Coteau, S.D. ;
Troubnikoff (Alexandre), *Les Martyrs de Lyon et leur temps*, O.E.I.L., Paris, 1986 ;
Voisin (Dominique), Guillet (Ginette), *La Soie, itinéraires en Rhône-Alpes*, Région Rhône-Alpes, 1989 ;
Wuilleumier (Pierre), *Lyon métropole des Gaules*, Société d'Edition Les Belles Lettres, Paris, 1953.

Revue *C'est 9 à Lyon*, revue municipale de Lyon ;
Revue *Lyon Cité*, revue municipale de Lyon ;
La soie, Rhône-Alpes, catalogue
Journal *Le Progrès*.

Achevé d'imprimer en janvier 2003
Dépôt légal 1er trimestre 2003
Printed in UE sur les presses de Beta